Looking Around

Paul Humphrey

Illustrated by

Maggie Downer

Evans

Let's look out for things in the
town on our way.

Look, a fire-engine!

Its siren is so loud!

6

The fire-engine is rushing to put out a fire.

7

The police-officers are talking
to the little girl.

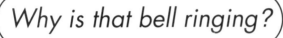

Some buildings have clocks
on them so that people can
tell the time.

Look, the post-woman is taking the letters out of the post-box.

She empties the post-box at 12 o'clock every day.

12

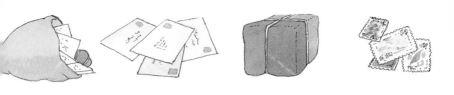

The letters are taken to be
sorted and delivered.

Here is the library.
I like borrowing books.

14

Dad brings me to the library for story time.

15

Every town has a town hall.
The people who run the town
work there.

The gardener is planting
some flowers.

20

There are ducks, swans and
cygnets on the pond.

Let's go and play by the statue.

22

Statues remind us about
famous people.

24

25

The ambulance is taking someone to hospital.

26

Nurses work hard to help sick people.

27

28

29

Here is a picture of the town.
Can you name all the people
and things we saw?